# 100 QUESTIONS about PIRATES

and all the answers too!

Written and Illustrated by
Simon Abbott

PETER PAUPER PRESS, INC.
White Plains, New York

## PETER PAUPER PRESS

In 1928, at the age of twenty-two, Peter Beilenson began printing books on a small press in the basement of his parents' home in Larchmont, New York. Peter—and later, his wife, Edna—sought to create fine books that sold at "prices even a pauper could afford."

Today, still family owned and operated, Peter Pauper Press continues to honor our founders' legacy of quality, value, and fun for big kids and small kids alike.

Designed by Heather Zschock

Text and illustrations copyright © 2018 by Simon Abbott

Published by Peter Pauper Press, Inc.
202 Mamaroneck Avenue
White Plains, New York 10601 USA

Published in the United Kingdom and Europe by Peter Pauper Press, Inc.
c/o White Pebble International
Unit 2, Plot 11 Terminus Rd.
Chichester, West Sussex PO19 8TX, UK

Library of Congress Cataloging-in-Publication Data Available

ISBN 978-1-4413-2615-7
Manufactured for Peter Pauper Press, Inc.
Printed in Hong Kong

7 6 5 4 3 2 1

Visit us at www.peterpauper.com

# AHOY THERE!

**For centuries,** pirates have crossed the oceans of the world, raiding treasure ships and capturing cargo.

**Were they fearless or ferocious?**
**Were they savage or were they smart?**
**Pirates were all of this and more!**
It's time to raise the anchor and begin our adventures on the seven seas.

Join us as we get the low-down on buried booty, fierce fights, painful punishments, and rotten rations.

Shake out your sea legs, dust off the map, and let's begin our voyage of discovery!

Welcome aboard, buccaneer!

AARRGGH!

# MEET THE CREW!

Pirates were fearless robbers who sailed the seas, raiding ships and getting up to no good! Jump on board and we'll introduce you to the cutthroat crew!

## What led honest folk down this crooked career path?

There were many different reasons. Some had been pirates from a young age, others were jobless sailors, and a few poor souls were forced to join the crew against their will.

## Let's take a roll call! Who's on board?

We'll start with the **captain**. He was elected by the crew and could be replaced by a show of hands, too. He usually had a servant or **cabin boy**.

## Who was next in command?

After the captain came the **quartermaster**. He would settle arguments, divide the loot, keep the accounts in order, and distribute food.

## Who was to blame if the boat drifted off course?

The **sailing master** was in charge of navigation.

## What did the boatswain do?

He was always on the go, making sure the sails and rigging were in working order and the decks were clean. He would also oversee the hoisting and dropping of the anchor. Phew!

## Did the boat have a carpenter?

Aye! This fellow would repair any damage to the hull or mast and plug any leaks in the sides of the ship, keeping it shipshape.

## Did the carpenter REALLY double up as the ship's surgeon?

I'm afraid so! He'd often perform operations and amputations with the same tools. *Yuck!*

# MOVING ON!

## Who would look after the guns and ammunition?

Introducing the **master gunner**. He'd be helped by the **powder monkey** who would run below deck to grab the gunpowder.

## What does A.B.S. stand for?

**Able-Bodied Sailor!** He was the backbone of the ship, and would know the vessel inside out!

The **swabbie** was the scalawag who had the tiresome task of mopping the decks.

## Were any jobs more dangerous than others?

The **rigger** had a treacherous job, and sometimes fell from the slippery masts and spars as the ship rocked and rolled over the sea.

# LIFE ABOARD!

It may have been smelly, cramped, and dangerous, but it was home! Let's take a pirate ship tour and discover life above and below deck.

## Who is Jolly Roger?
It's not a person! It's a pirate flag, often featuring the skull and crossbones.

**Rigging:** The ropes and chains used to support the masts and arrange the sails

## What is the stern?
The name for the back of the ship

**Rudder:** An underwater blade used to turn the boat

## Where is the quarterdeck?
This raised deck is behind the main mast

**Stores:** These items are found on the lower decks. Food, water, beer, gunpowder, cannonballs, spare sails, and ropes are kept here.

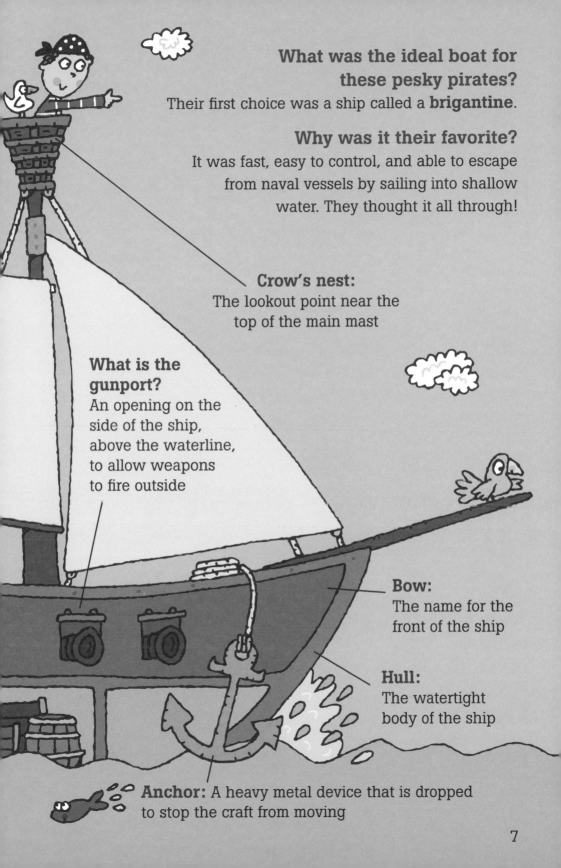

**What was the ideal boat for these pesky pirates?**
Their first choice was a ship called a **brigantine**.

**Why was it their favorite?**
It was fast, easy to control, and able to escape from naval vessels by sailing into shallow water. They thought it all through!

**Crow's nest:**
The lookout point near the top of the main mast

**What is the gunport?**
An opening on the side of the ship, above the waterline, to allow weapons to fire outside

**Bow:**
The name for the front of the ship

**Hull:**
The watertight body of the ship

**Anchor:** A heavy metal device that is dropped to stop the craft from moving

## Where did the crew sleep?

Most pirates dozed in hammocks hung from the ceilings of the decks. These hammocks would rock and sway with the movement of the ship, and give them a good night's sleep. Zzzzz!

## Was that as cozy as it sounds?

Not always! Conditions were cramped, so occasionally shipmates had to bed down on a bag of corn or try to find a dry patch on the floor.

## Did the captain have his own place to call home?

Yes! The boss had his own quarters, with a comfortable bunk. His cabin would be a place to entertain guests, dine with the senior crew, and spread out his maps.

**And where were the bathrooms?**
You're joking! There were no showers, baths, or washbasins.
Pirates would STINK! Fresh water would be reserved for drinking
only, so if the stench was too bad they'd slop a bucket of seawater
over themselves.  Shiver me timbers!

**You know what's coming. How did this smelly squad
relieve themselves?**
Glad you asked!  At the bow of the ship, there was a space in the floor
called the **head**. Shipmates would squat over this hole, and their
pirate poos would splash into the sea below.  The crew would urinate
in buckets, or simply aim over the side of the boat!

WATCH OUT BELOW!

DO NOT DISTURB

**Did these stinky seafarers climb down from the
crow's nest if they needed the john?**
It wasn't worth the effort! What a pity their shipmates
below didn't carry umbrellas!

Where do pirates keep their bathrooms?

On the poop deck!

# ROTTEN RATIONS AND MOLDY MEALS!

With bugs in the biscuits and maggots in the meat, a pirate's menu might leave you feeling hungry. Dinner is served!

## Did pirates take turns cooking to test out their recipes?

No. The ship usually had a cook, often known as **slouchy**. This role would be filled by an injured seaman, who may have lost an eye or a limb.

## Where did the cook chop, slice, and bake the meals?

The kitchen or **galley** was usually found toward the stern of the ship. A fire would be built in a sandbox, and the floor lined with tin to prevent hot coals from starting a fire. Very sensible!

Pickled Pig

## Pirates sometimes sailed for months on end. How did the ship's cook keep the food fresh?

Livestock such as pigs, cattle, sheep, goats, and chickens were sometimes kept on deck and cooked when required. However, space was extremely limited, so meat was often dried, salted, and kept in barrels.

## Did the crew enjoy plenty of fruit and vegetables?

I'm afraid not. The vegetables they did have were either pickled or dried. It was impossible to protect fresh produce from bugs and rats.

## Sounds terrible! Was their diet particularly unhealthy?

It certainly was! The lack of vitamin C on a pirate's menu meant that they often got scurvy, a disease that could cause death if untreated.

## Wait, if pirates died, then how were funerals handled at sea?

If a pirate died aboard ship, the body would be washed by his mates, dressed in his best suit, and wrapped up in a sheet. Then weights would be added to sink the corpse. Farewell, old seadog!

**They were surrounded by sea. Surely they could catch something to eat?**

Of course! The seafarers caught fish, eels, and particularly enjoyed the occasional sea turtle. If buccaneers were hard-pressed, they had to rely on desperate rations. **Captain Henry Morgan** and his pirates dined on a meal of chopped and fried leather satchels, while **Captain Charlotte de Berry**'s shipwrecked crew once ate Charlotte's husband!

What do pirates put on their toast?

jelly Roger!

**Can you describe a pirate's favorite meal?**
It's hard to pick one, but **salmagundi** was a very popular salad dish.
In a buccaneer's recipe from 1712 the ingredients featured (deep
breath!) turtle meat, chicken, pork, beef, ham, pigeon, fish, spiced
wine, cabbage, anchovies, pickled herring, mango, hard boiled eggs,
onions, olives, grapes, garlic, chili pepper, mustard, salt, and pepper.

*Phew!*

**What delicacy *didn't* meet with the pirates' approval?**
At the bottom of the pile is the **hardtack**. It was a biscuit made with
flour, water, and salt, and was extremely hard and dry. It could be
kept for a year, and pirates chose to eat it in the dark so they couldn't
see the mold and crawling insects. That's one tough cookie!

# PARTY LIKE A PIRATE!

**Climb down from the crow's nest and put away the mop.
It's time to stretch your sea legs and celebrate!**

**We all love a party! Who were the most popular
folks on board a pirate ship?**
The musicians! They would play at meal times and dances.
The crew's favorites were jigs and sea shanties.

## What is a sea shanty?
A work song! It can also be spelled "chantey," and comes
from the French word "chanter," which means "to sing."
The rhythm of the songs helped shipmates as they raised the
anchor or hauled up the sails. In battle, the musicians played
loud, crashing military music to frighten the enemy.

## Did pirates play sports?

Well, ball games on board were out of the question, as you can imagine! Racing, however, was always popular. Sailors would bet on the fastest runner around the deck, or the quickest climber to the top of the mast.

Why didn't anyone want to play cards with the pirate?

Because he was standing on the deck.

## So, they liked to gamble?

They would wager on anything and everything, from dice and card games to chicken races and rapid rats. Place your bets!

## There is a rumor that pirates MAY have enjoyed the odd sip of rum. Can this be true?

Yo ho ho! It's likely that pirates were rarely sober! The water was not always safe to drink, so ale was the preferred refreshment. To help them through the day, they would also be given a shot or two of something stronger, so by sunset the crew would be quite merry. *Aarrgghh!*

## I'm surprised they could stand up! Were they all wild and woozy?

Some were worse than others. A German pirate was nicknamed **Stortebeker**, which means "empty the mug with one swallow." His party trick was to empty an eight-pint tankard of beer in one gulp. Hic!

## What an unhealthy bunch! Are there any other nasty habits we should know about?

Well, there was a bit of a tobacco problem. While the risk of fire meant there was no smoking below deck, a pirate would puff on a clay pipe on the top deck, or often chew his tobacco ration.

## Gambling! Drinking! Smoking! Do we have any examples of good clean fun?

There were the mock trials. Pirates would each take the part of a lawyer, judge, jury, jailer, and hangman. The crew would have great fun arresting the "criminal," then have him tried and "hanged" for his made-up crime.

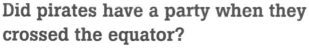

## Did pirates have a party when they crossed the equator?

Good question! Firstly, the equator is an imaginary line around the middle of the planet. When a pirate ship crossed the equator, a ceremony would be performed. Mean tricks would be played on buccaneers who were crossing the line for the first time.

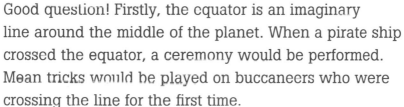

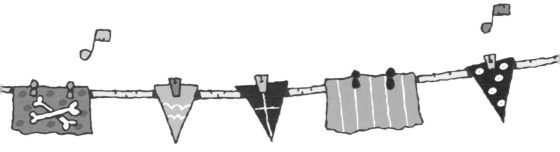

### Such as?

A new pirate would be attached to a wooden spar, then hauled high above the ocean. The poor fellow would then be repeatedly dunked in the sea. Alternatively, the shipmate would be submerged several times in a barrel of seawater.

# TERRIFIC TREASURE!

It's time to dig deep and uncover the tales of buried silver and hidden jewels. Where did pirates strike gold, and who got lucky with their loot?

## We know all about gold and silver.
## What other loot did these sea villains like to pinch?

It may sound obvious, but the short answer is ANYTHING they could sell, use, or eat! This could include fine fabrics, tobacco, snuff, weapons, ammunition, rum, wine, sugar, and coffee. Medicine was valuable, too!

## Medicine! Why was that so valuable?

Pirates sometimes became ill or injured, and pills and potions were hard to get ahold of. In fact, when the famous pirate Blackbeard held the city of Charleston (in South Carolina) hostage, his only ransom demand was a chest of medicine!

*Aye!*

## How did pirates divide the loot?

The method of splitting the treasure was set out in the pirate code. It was up to the ship's quartermaster to divide the treasure, and this was usually completed without challenge.

## What did the pirates spend their swag on?

Pirates weren't known for their savings accounts! Tavern landlords would happily relieve these scoundrels of their loot. Once ashore, rum would be ordered, and they would gamble away their ill-gotten gains.

# Where were the best places to strike it lucky?

Roll out the map and take a look!

## Here are the top tips...

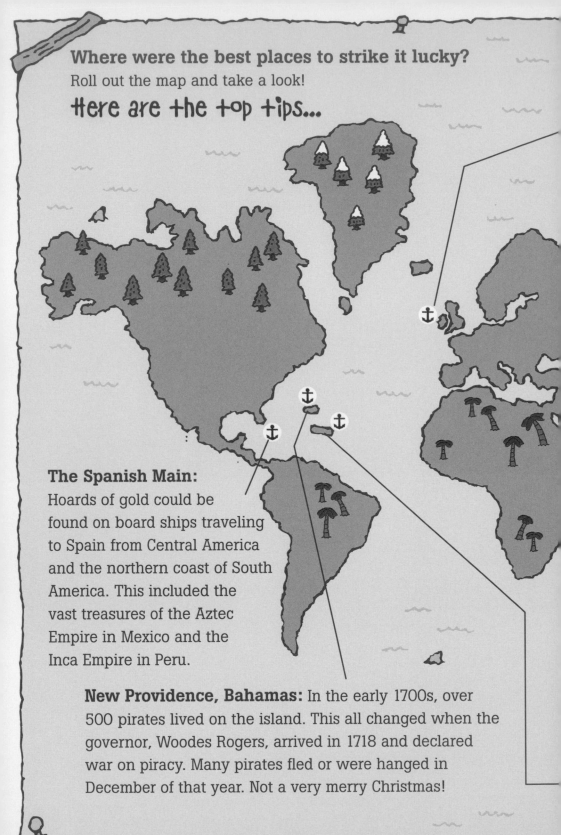

**The Spanish Main:**
Hoards of gold could be
found on board ships traveling
to Spain from Central America
and the northern coast of South
America. This included the
vast treasures of the Aztec
Empire in Mexico and the
Inca Empire in Peru.

**New Providence, Bahamas:** In the early 1700s, over
500 pirates lived on the island. This all changed when the
governor, Woodes Rogers, arrived in 1718 and declared
war on piracy. Many pirates fled or were hanged in
December of that year. Not a very merry Christmas!

## Any hot spots in Europe?
**Clew Bay** in Ireland was the stronghold for **Grace O'Malley,** an intimidating and infamous lady pirate. From her base at Rockfleet Castle she led hundreds of men in raids on merchant ships and rival clans.

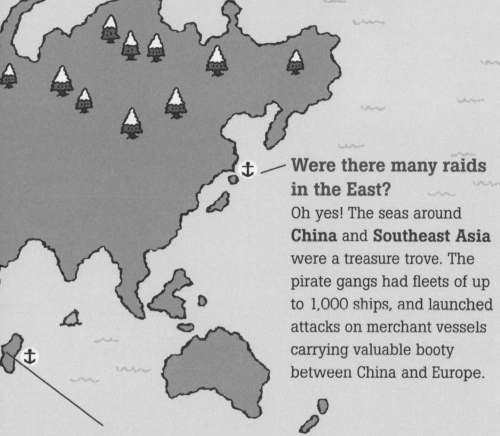

## Were there many raids in the East?
Oh yes! The seas around **China** and **Southeast Asia** were a treasure trove. The pirate gangs had fleets of up to 1,000 ships, and launched attacks on merchant vessels carrying valuable booty between China and Europe.

## What is this island called?
**Madagascar:** Villains would plunder ships for their precious cargos of spice on this island.

**Port Royal, Jamaica:** In the mid-1600s the island's governors offered the port as a safe haven for pirates, in exchange for protection against the Spanish.

**Did pirates REALLY bury their treasure?**
Very rarely. **William Kidd** is one of the very few known to have buried his loot. He deposited some gold and jewels on Gardiners Island, New York. Kidd was hoping that his knowledge of this treasure trove would give him an easy ride once he was captured. No such luck! He was sentenced to death in 1701.

**So, no treasure maps either, then?**
I'm afraid not! Rather than bury their haul, pirates would spend it, then move onto the next raid.

What's the difference between a pirate and a cranberry farmer?

the pirate buries his treasure, and the farmer treasures his berries.

**Blimey! No buried chests?
No treasure maps?
Give me some good news!
Which pirates really hit the jackpot?**
**Henry Avery** did VERY well for himself.
In 1695 he captured the ships *Fateh Muhammed*
and *Ganj-i-sawai* in the Arabian Sea.
After hours of ferocious fighting, the pirates were
victorious. Avery had plundered up to $600,000 in
precious metals and jewels, which is worth over
$121,000,000 today. That's some paycheck!

**Were all pirates crooks and criminals?**
Some felt they were on the right side of the
law. The greedy rulers of England and France
granted permits to a few pirates, which gave
them permission to attack the Spanish fleets.

# PIRATES ON PARADE!

Let's peek inside a pirate's wardrobe! What would these scoundrels pack for their adventures on the ocean waves?

## Is it true that pirates wore eye patches?

Yes, they did! Pirates would wear patches so that one eye would be prepared for the gloom below deck. This was very useful in a fight on board ship, when the pirate would move quickly from daylight to darkness.

## How many shoes did a pirate own?

Usually none! Bare feet would grip a slippery deck or ladder much better than shoes.

## Why did pirates wear gold earrings?

If a poor pirate died at sea, the earring could be used as money to pay for a proper burial. Some pirates even believed that piercing their ear with silver or gold would improve their eyesight!

Which pirate wears the biggest hat?

the one with the biggest head.

## What sort of hat did a pirate actually wear?

Ordinary pirates wore knitted caps, as anything else would be blown off in a storm. When ashore, pirate captains might wear cocked hats, decorated with jewelry and feathers. Fancy!

**Very important question!
What sort of underpants did
pirates wear?**
They didn't wear any! Pirates would tuck
in their long shirt tails as protection against
their itchy woolen trousers. Sounds like a
good idea!

FACT OR FICTION?

**Did pirates REALLY have wooden
legs and hooks for hands?**
Yes! Pirate ships were dangerous places. Not only
were pirates injured in fights, but they tumbled
down hatches and fell from high masts. Crushed
limbs had to be amputated and a wooden leg or
hook was fitted instead. *Aarrgghh!*

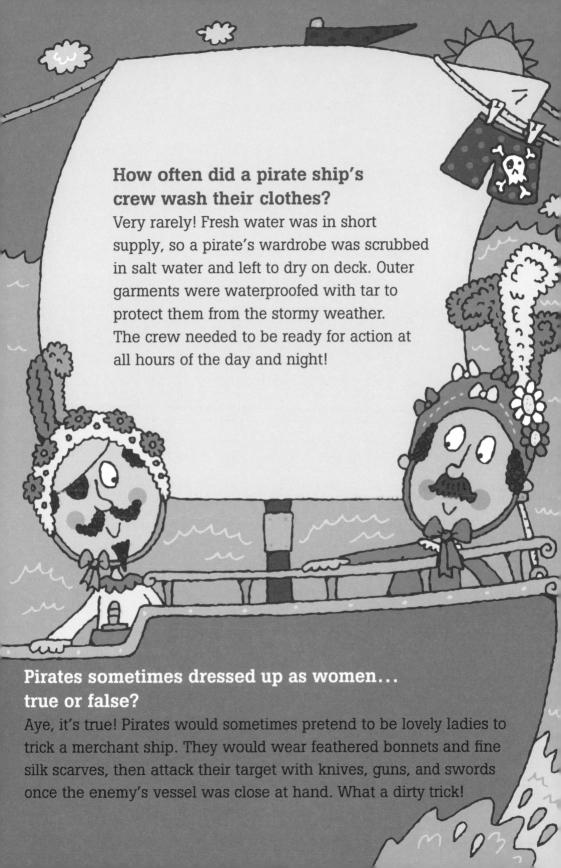

## How often did a pirate ship's crew wash their clothes?

Very rarely! Fresh water was in short supply, so a pirate's wardrobe was scrubbed in salt water and left to dry on deck. Outer garments were waterproofed with tar to protect them from the stormy weather. The crew needed to be ready for action at all hours of the day and night!

## Pirates sometimes dressed up as women… true or false?

Aye, it's true! Pirates would sometimes pretend to be lovely ladies to trick a merchant ship. They would wear feathered bonnets and fine silk scarves, then attack their target with knives, guns, and swords once the enemy's vessel was close at hand. What a dirty trick!

# PIRATE TALK?
## WELL, BLOW ME DOWN!

Pirates chatted to their chums with their own private lingo. Let's get you up to speed with this dastardly dictionary!

**What word would I use to hail a ship or a person?**
Ahoy!

**If I wanted to have a conversation with the enemy, and halt the skirmish?**
Parley!

**Someone has offered me some Nelson's folly. Should I accept it?**
You'll have to say "no." It's rum!

**I want to wake up a sleeping pirate. What should I shout?**
Show a leg!

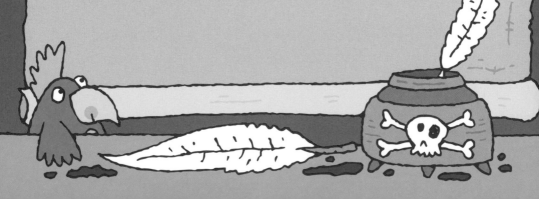

**A captured captain is about to "dance the hempen jig." What's going to happen?**
He's going to be hanged. Gulp!

**What is Davy Jones' Locker?**
A phrase used to describe the mythical watery grave everyone goes to when they die at sea.

**If I was to "kiss the gunner's daughter" would that be a nice experience?**
Ah, no. You'd be hoisted over a ship's gun and flogged. Ouch!

**Finally, I'm going to "take a caulk." What would I be doing?**
You'd be having a snooze! The gap between the deck's planks were filled with rope and black tar, called caulk. If a pirate fell asleep on deck he could be left with a telltale black streak down his back when he woke up!

What would you call a pirate with no eye?

A PRATE.

# BRUTAL BATTLES AND RISKY RAIDS

These merciless marauders knew how to pick a fight. It's time to duck and dive and discover their swashbuckling secrets!

## What equipment did these scoundrels grab to maim and murder?

Their go-to sword would be the **cutlass**. This had a short, curved blade that made it ideal for fighting in a ship's cramped quarters.

## What if the cutlass wasn't available?

Next on the list would be the **boarding axe**. This versatile implement allowed a pirate to climb the sides of a ship and chop through the rigging. They could hack through doors and hatches in the blink of an eye, and give an opponent a severe headache, too!

FACT OR FICTION?

## Did pirates ever use guns?

Aye! **Muskets** were developed in the 17th century, and were used in boarding raids. The **blunderbuss** was a wide-bore shotgun with a flared muzzle. This was a savage short-range weapon, scattering lead balls in a wide arc at the enemy.

The lightweight **flintlock pistol** was a favorite of the pirates. It took so long to reload, however, that pirates often carried several, tied to their belts with silk cord to stop them from dropping overboard! Blackbeard supposedly carried six!

## How heavy were cannonballs?

They were all sizes, from two to thirty-two pounds (1 to 15 kg). That's almost as heavy as a toddler!

## Silly question! Did cannons just fire cannonballs?

No! They'd fire almost anything to cause maximum damage to the opponent's boat and crew. Scrap iron, nails, spikes, and even gold coins were used as missiles, and grappling hooks were fired to enable the rival boat to be pulled closer. Pirate power!

## What's a stinkpot?
## Is that an early ocean-going restroom?

Wrong! These were small, round containers filled with sulfur and occasionally rotten fish. They were lit, then slung onto the decks of the enemy boat. The foul-smelling fumes would cause panic, confusion, and a stampede to the side of the ship to barf!

**Let's put these weapons into action!**
**Who had a dangerous display of firepower?**
**Benjamin Hornigold** was a peculiar pirate! He began his criminal career around 1713 with just a handful of canoes, and within a couple of years had upgraded to a 30-gun warship! He overtook and raided a merchant ship in Honduras, Central America, in this well-equipped gunboat.

**What kind of loot did Hornigold plunder?**
Hats! All he demanded from crew and passengers were hats! His crew had gotten drunk the night before and had tossed their own headgear overboard. I take my hat off to him!

Where do pirates put their weapons?

In their enemies.

## Who wins the prize for the most merciless marauder?

The gold medal goes to the pitiless pirate, **Edward Low**. He was the most feared villain of the early 1700s.

## Why was Low feared?

Here goes, but turn the page if you're feeling squeamish!

He'd think nothing of tying a victim's arms behind his back, then placing rope between each finger. Low would then set the rope on fire and watch the flames toast the prisoner. Blimey!

Rare, medium rare, or well done?

## That's terrible! Was he REALLY that ruthless?

Without question! Low would use all kinds of gruesome torture methods, including grilling people—literally!

# PUNISHMENT FOR PIRATES!

There's always payback for bad behavior, even among a crew of rotten rascals. What were the consequences if a pirate stepped out of line?  Let's see how the captain kept order!

## From what we have heard, pirates were an unruly rabble. Did they REALLY have rules and regulations?

Well, even scoundrels have standards! Each crew had their own **pirate code** instructing them how they should behave.

## What rules were included?

Each pirate code was slightly different, but it covered guidelines on voting for the captain, compensation for the loss of limbs, dividing the loot, and more.

## Were wicked pirates REALLY forced to walk the plank?

It's fiction! There is no proof that this punishment existed. After all, if a pirate wanted to drown a shipmate they could simply throw them overboard. Heave-ho!

## So, what alternative punishments could be handed out?

A penalty that seafarers dreaded was to be **marooned**, sometimes teaching a lesson to a captured sailor who refused to join the pirate crew. The victim would be left on a deserted island with just a bottle of water and a pistol with powder and shot. He had no food, and no protection against wild animals or hungry sharks. He'd get pretty lonesome, too!

## Shiver me timbers! That sounds quite harsh! Was there anything worse?

**Keelhauling** was a particularly gruesome punishment, reserved for murderers and thieves. A rope would be attached to the pirate then looped beneath the boat. The poor fellow would be dragged under the vessel as it sailed onward.

### What is the cat-o'-nine tails?

It's not a strange pet! The **cat-o'-nine tails** was a whip, made by unwinding nine strands at the end of a rope, and was used to crack down on disobedient pirates. Even worse, the whipping wounds were occasionally covered with salt and vinegar to increase the pain. *Ouch!*

### How were pirates disciplined by *sweating*?

First of all, it didn't involve sitting in a sauna! This torture involved the crew stabbing, prodding, and poking the victim with knives or cutlasses. The pirate tried to duck and dodge to escape the attack, which was a challenge as he was tied to the mast by a short rope. This torture was sometimes used to force merchant ship captains to reveal the location of their hidden treasure. That's not fair!

## How were quarrels settled on board ship?
## Did they hug and say sorry?

Because they didn't bathe much, a hug would not be recommended!
If a pirate stole from a fellow shipmate, the thief would have his
nose and ear slit, then ordered off the vessel. If two pirates had a
disagreement, it would be resolved by a duel with pistols once
ashore. If both pirates missed, the argument would be settled with
cutlasses. The shipmate to draw the first blood was the winner.
Case dismissed!

# STARS OF THE SEA!

Which plundering pirates were making headlines as they sailed the world's oceans? Let's take a stroll to the Pirates' Hall of Fame!

## Who was the most fearsome looking pirate?

That award would go to Edward Teach, better known as **Blackbeard**.

FACT OR FICTION?

## Did he REALLY have a black beard?

Yes! He never shaved, so he had an enormous black beard and long black hair. In battle, he filled his beard with slow-burning fuses that sparked and smoked, giving him an extremely fierce appearance.

## Sounds terrifying!
## So Blackbeard was a bit of a tough guy?

He certainly was! Even when his end came, he didn't give up easily. In 1718, British naval officers hunted him down. After suffering 25 wounds (including five from gunshots), he finally died.

## Was that the end of the story?

Not quite! British Lieutenant Maynard needed proof of the pirate's demise in order to claim the reward for Blackbeard's death. He beheaded the notorious pirate, and hung his head from the front of his ship on the voyage home.

## Who were the other pirate celebrities?

**Captain Henry Morgan** was an extremely successful pirate on the Spanish Main. His most famous raid was in Panama, where he captured over 100,000 pounds of stolen treasure. His evildoings were ignored back home in Britain, and King Charles II knighted him in 1674. Arise, Sir Morgan!

**Sounds like he had a lucky escape! Were there any other pesky pirates who avoided punishment?**

Let me introduce **Cheung Po Tsai.** He was adopted by a pirate, and took up piracy himself, eventually commanding an army of 50,000 men and hundreds of ships. He kept his vast hoard of treasure in a small cave, which is now named after him. He struck a deal with the Chinese government, which pardoned him, and he joined the Qing Imperial Navy. He reached the rank of colonel and spent the rest of his life capturing other pirates. Shiver me timbers!

**Who was François l'Olonnais?**

You might want to keep well clear, as he was a bloodthirsty French buccaneer! He raided towns, captured ships, and following one attack in Venezuela, fled with 260,000 Spanish dollars, plus silverware, silk, and jewels. Once, when frustrated by a Spanish prisoner's silence, he cut out his heart and began to chew it! He didn't miss a beat!

Bon appétit.

## What brutal behavior!
## Did pirates always get away with it?

Not at all! In 1698, the Scottish pirate **Captain William Kidd** attacked an East India Company ship. This was a mistake, as they were a large and influential trading firm. Kidd was now a wanted man. He was captured, sent back to England, and sentenced to be hanged. During the hanging, the noose broke twice, but Kidd was killed on the third attempt. His body was covered in tar, and he was hung in a cage along the River Thames.

## So, who shall we crown as
## King of the Pirates?

Step to, matey! That title is awarded to **Bartholomew "Black Bart" Roberts**. His pirate ship, the *Royal Fortune*, was well-armed, with 26 formidable cannons. In just three years following 1719, he terrorized the seas, attacking, capturing, and robbing over 400 merchant ships. He was cruel, cunning, and courageous, and he takes the number one star on the pirate walk of fame.

# GRUESOME GIRLS!

It's time to heave the guys overboard! Female pirates were a force to be reckoned with, as you are about to find out. Who were these light-fingered ladies?

## Female pirates seem quite sparse in numbers. Why is that?

It was sometimes thought that having a woman on board a pirate ship was bad luck and would anger the sea gods!

## So this is mainly based on superstition?

Aye, and it was strictly enforced. The pirate Bartholomew Roberts wrote in his pirate code that, "No woman is allowed amongst them. If any man is found carrying her out to sea in disguise he shall suffer death."

Cheers, Mary!

FACT OR FICTION?

## So there were NEVER any female pirates?

That's pure fiction. Of course there were female pirates. Let's start with **Anne Bonny**. She joined "Calico Jack" Rackham's crew, and fought under his command. She dressed, acted, brawled, and drank just like any man on board.

## Was she the only woman on board?

No! As luck would have it, she was soon joined by a fellow female pirate, **Mary Read**. She had been captured by Calico Jack too, and eventually began to enjoy the pirate way of life. Mary and Anne became great friends.

ROTTEN RAIDS LEADER BOARD
1. ANNE IIIII IIIII IIIII IIIII
2. MARY IIIII IIIII IIIII I
3. PEG-LEG PETE IIII
4. HOOK-HAND HARRY III
5. ONE-EYED WILSON I

What would you call a lady pirate wirth 4 eyes?

A piiiirate!

**Onward! How did the pirate Sadie Farrell earn the name "Sadie the Goat"?**

Is it due to her two horns and a furry beard? No! It's because she head-butted her victims when stealing from them. She also lost an ear when fellow female thug **Gallus Mag** bit it off in a brawl. Ouch!

**That sounds gruesome! Was Sadie's ear gone for good?**

Gallus Mag had kept the ear pickled, and returned it to Sadie once they had made their peace. Sadie placed the ear in a locket and wore it around her neck for the rest of her life.

## Who was "Back from the Dead Red"?

First, see if you can say her name, very quickly, ten times in a row. (Well done!)

Her real name was **Jacquotte Delahaye**. She stole a fortune and inspired many storytellers. Her title comes from a tale that claimed this red-haired pirate faked her own death to escape capture in the 1660s. She disguised herself as a man and took on a new identity. When the dust had settled, she re-emerged with her catchy nickname "Back from the Dead Red."

## Who wins first prize as the pirate queen?

The champion is **Ching Shih** (also known as Cheng I Sao), who in the 19th century sailed the China Sea. She ran her Red Flag Fleet with a strict code of conduct, and if a pirate stole a single penny from her treasury, she would think nothing of chopping off his head and dumping the body in the ocean. Sounds brutal!

## Did she ever get caught and punished?

Ching Shih was a cunning operator and negotiated a deal with the Chinese government. She and her forces were allowed to retire and keep all their plundered loot. What a gal!

# LIES AND LEGENDS!

Over time, the pirates' adventures have been embellished and exaggerated. Let's help you sort the facts from the fibs!

### Did all pirate flags feature the skull and crossbones?

No! Pirates flew flags with many different designs, some in just a single color of black or red.

### Many pirate captains had their own flags. Have you got an example?

Of course! Evil Edward Low's banner displayed a blood-red skeleton on a black background. Those who saw this flag knew a frightful fate awaited them!

## Did pirates sink every ship they encountered and slaughter everyone on board?

To be honest, no! Usually a merchant ship would surrender with just a glimpse of a pirate flag and a pirate's warning shot fired.

## Would they be sent on their way without a care in the world?

The pirate quartermaster might ask the merchant ship's crew if their captain was a satisfactory skipper. If he turned out to be mean, the pirates might torture or even hang him. If he was given a fair report, he and his crew would be given a small ship and were free to go!

# AHOY! Let's talk about parrots!
## Were they really kept as pets?

Look at it this way. Greedy sea raiders loved money, and these exotic birds from the Caribbean were valuable in Europe. These colorful creatures would be captured, then sold in European cities, to line the pirates' pockets.

What's orange and sounds like a parrot?

A carrot.

## Are pirates now dead and buried? Have they all disappeared into history?

Far from it! Modern pirates are active today. They have night-vision goggles instead of eye patches, and rocket launchers instead of muskets. It is estimated that losses from worldwide piracy may be as high as $16 billion. Shiver me timbers!